Summary
of

Discrimination and Disparities
Thomas Sowell

Conversation Starters

By Paul Adams
Book Habits

Tips for Using Conversation Starters:

EVERY GOOD BOOK CONTAINS A WORLD FAR DEEPER THAN the surface of its pages. Questions herein are designed to bring us beneath the surface of the page and invite us into the world that lives on. These questions can be used to:

- Foster a deeper understanding of the book
- Promote an atmosphere of discussion for groups
- Assist in the study of the book, either individually or corporately
- Explore unseen realms of the book as never seen before

Table of Contents

Introducing *Discrimination and Disparities*

homas Sowell's latest book *Discrimination and Disparities* is about the different economic outcomes of different individuals, groups and their nations. There are many scholars who offered their perspective on the matter but no one has done it better than Thomas Sowell. In this short book, a few pages short of 200, Thomas Sowell disproves the myths that have been widely believed not just in the United States but all around the globe.

One of these myths is about discrimination: the fact that if not for discrimination, everyone will be represented proportionately in various socio-economic characteristics. These characteristics include career, education, income, and incarceration. Sowell argues that the fact is, there is no found evidence that illustrates that at any time in history, but for the fact of discrimination, there would be a proportionate representation of everyone by nationality, race, sex, or any other human characteristic. Sowell writes that socio-economic outcomes become widely varied depending on the individuals, or groups or nation that is involved. They differ in ways that cannot be explained by just one factor, whether it's discrimination, genetics or any form of exploitation.

A study was conducted on National Merit Scholarship finalists and it showed that most of the finalists are firstborns. This happens more often than the combination of their multiple siblings. Additionally, data was gathered from Germany, Britain and United States that showed that the average IQ of firstborns is relatively higher than the average IQ of the siblings that came after them. Such outcomes of studies challenge the myths that a child's environment or heredity is the dominant and determining factor for his or her academic performance. In light of these findings, Sowell argues that if equality cannot be found among people born to the same set of parents and are living under the same roof, 'why should equality of outcomes be expected under other conditions?'

In the book's second chapter, Sowell provides significant evidence that people would not take racial discrimination at any given cost. The higher the cost given, the less will racial discrimination be tolerated and vice versa. One example he gave was the segregated seating on a particular municipal transit in the South. Many companies were privately run and privately owned. The decision makers of these companies understand that there is a big possibility that they could lose profits when the establishment of segregated seating offends their black customers. A number of transportation companies have fought against the laws that mandated the segregated seating depending on races but they lost. Some companies tried to ignore the law but when they were faced with fines, they began to comply.

Sowell says that the difference between the white politicians and other segregationists from the white transportation owners was the transportation company owners would shoulder the cost of alienating the black riders and the former would not. Sowell broadens his arguments and says that regulated organizations and companies, like public utilities and nonprofit entities like government agencies and colleges, will be at the forefront when it's popular to discriminate against blacks. They will also be at the forefront when what's popular to do is to discriminate in favor of blacks. The reason is because they would not shoulder the burden of gone profits. In the chapter *The World of Numbers*, Sowell points out dishonesty.

In the year 2000, a study conducted by the U.S. Commission on Civil Rights showed that 44.6 percent of mortgage requests of black applicants were rejected. But only 22.3 percent of white applicants were turned down. Asian and native Hawaiian applicants had a lower percentage of 12.4 percent. Other similar characteristics lead to charges of discrimination in the lending industry. These statistics do not see the light of day because they do not fit the narrative on racial discrimination. Sowell also cites the tragedies created for the pursuit of social justice. He writes about the Gujaratis and how they were expelled from Uganda and the Cubans who fled Cuba. Many of the Gujaratis who arrived in Britain were once destitute but they stood up again and rose to prosperity. Cubans who came to the United States also prospered. Because they lost their most productive people, Uganda and Cuba became cases of economic basket.

The Conservative Woman praises Sowell's writing and says that he writes "in a manner that is not only accessible, but also relevant and even riveting." *American Thinker* says that only a few works can "maintain such a consistent focus on empirical evidence while avoiding rhetorical jabs at opponents." *New York Journal of Books* praises Thomas Sowell and says that his work "calmly but persuasively shatter myths and ideological beliefs about race, ethnicity, economics, history, and culture."

Discussion Questions

"Get Ready to Enter a New World"

Tip: Begin with questions dealing with broader issues to ensure ample time for quality discussions. Read through all discussion questions before engaging.

~~~

question 1

Author Thomas Sowell breaks myths in his latest book *Discrimination and Disparities.* One of the myths is that if not for discrimination, everyone will be represented proportionately in various socio-economic characteristics. What are the different socio-economic factors?

~~~

~~~

question 2

Socio-economic outcomes become widely varied depending on the individuals, or groups or nation that is involved. They differ in ways that cannot be explained by just one factor. What are the three factors that people usually point to regarding different socio-economic outcomes?

~~~

~~~

question 3

Data was gathered from Germany, Britain and United States that showed that the average IQ of firstborns is relatively higher than the average IQ of the siblings that came after them. Why do firstborns usually have higher IQ than his or her siblings?

~~~

~~~

question 4

The myths that a child's environment or heredity is the dominant and determining factor for his or her academic performance. What arguments did Sowell present against this myth?

~~~

~ ~ ~

question 5

Many companies were privately run and privately owned. The decision makers of these companies were not in favor of racial discrimination. What could possibly happen to their company if the segregated seating was enforced?

~ ~ ~

question 6

Some transportation companies tried to ignore the law but when they were faced with fines, they began to comply. What does this trend say about people's tolerance of racial discrimination?

question 7

White politicians and other segregationists together with white transportation owners complied with the law but Sowell says there is a big difference between the transportation owners and the former. What was that difference?

~~~

~~~

question 8

Sowell observes that government agencies and colleges are always at the forefront when it's popular to discriminate against blacks. They will also be at the forefront when what's popular to do is to discriminate in favor of blacks. Why is this so?

~~~

question 9

Sowell says that regulated organizations and companies advocate racial discrimination whether it's against a certain race or for it. Which regulated companies is Thomas Sowell pertaining to?

~ ~ ~

~~~

question 10

A study conducted by the U.S. Commission on Civil Rights showed that 44.6 percent of mortgage requests of black applicants were rejected. But only 22.3 percent of white applicants were turned down. What does this statistic imply regarding racial discrimination?

~~~

~~~

question 11

The study also showed that the rejection of mortgage requests of Asian and native Hawaiian applicants had a lower percentage of 12.4 percent. According to Sowell, why doesn't this statistic see the light of day?

~~~

question 12

Sowell also cites the tragedies created for the pursuit of social justice. He writes about the Gujaratis and how they were expelled from Uganda. What is the case of the Gujaratis? Why were they expelled from Uganda?

~~~

~ ~ ~

question 13

Another tragedy created for the pursuit of social justice is the time when the Cubans fled from Cuba. Why did the Cubans flee their country?

~ ~ ~

~~~

question 14

Many of the Gujaratis who arrived in Britain were once destitute but they stood up again and rose to prosperity. How did the destitute Gujaratis immigrants thrive in Britain?

~~~

question 15

Thomas Sowell says that because they lost their most productive people, Uganda and Cuba became cases of economic basket. What is an economic basket?

~~~

question 16

The Conservative Woman praises Sowell's writing and says that he writes "in a manner that is not only accessible, but also relevant and even riveting." Describe Sowell's manner of writing. How does he make his lofty arguments accessible to his readers?

~~~

~~~

question 17

American Thinker says that only a few works can "maintain such a consistent focus on empirical evidence while avoiding rhetorical jabs at opponents." How did Sowell maintain his focus on a highly controversial topic?

~~~

~~~

question 18

New York Journal of Books praises Thomas Sowell and says that his work "calmly but persuasively shatter myths and ideological beliefs about race, ethnicity, economics, history, and culture." How does Sowell calmly shatter myths and beliefs?

~~~

~~~

question 19

Washington Times praises Sowell's book and describes it as "sane, balanced and highly informed discussion." How did Sowell maintain a balanced take on the matter of discrimination?

~~~

question 20

Power Line praises Dr. Thomas Sowell and says that everything he writes is worth reading. He continues to say that this book "couldn't be more timely." What current events is answered by this book?

Introducing the Author

Author Thomas Sowell is a social theorist and economist. Sowell was born in 1930 in his family home in Gastonia, North Carolina. Shortly before his birth, his father died. His mother worked as a housemaid. Sowell was born after her four children. His great aunt and her two adult daughters adopted and raised Sowell when he was young. When Sowell was nine years old, his family moved to North Carolina, then to New York as part of the African Americans' Great Migration from the South to the North in search for greater opportunities. His intelligence qualified him for a prestigious academic high school in New York City, Stuyvesant High School. He was the first in his clan to study further than the sixth grade. However, when he was 17 years old, he was forced to drop out because of financial and domestic difficulties.

Sowell started working different jobs at Western Union and at a machine shop. In 1948, he tried out for a position at the Brooklyn Dodgers. In 1951, he was drafted into the military. He served during the Korean War. He was assigned in the United States Marine Corps. Sowell became a Marine Corps photographer.

After his discharge, Sowell worked in Washington D.C. in civil service position. While working, he attended the night classes at Howard

University. The high scores he earned on the College Board exams together with the recommendations from two of his professors helped him in his admission to Harvard University.

In 1958, he received his Bachelor's Degree in Economics from Harvard University. He graduated with the honors of magna cum laude. In 1959, he studied in Columbia University for his Master's degree. In 1968, he graduated from University of Chicago and received his Doctor of Philosophy degree in Economics. His doctoral dissertation was entitled *Say's Law and the General Glut Controversy.* Sowell's initial choice for a university was Columbia University. He wanted to study under George Stigler, a recipient of the Nobel Prize in Economics.

However, when he learned that George Stigler already moved to the University of Chicago, he decided to follow him there.

Thomas Sowell has served as part of the faculty at several universities. These universities include University of California in Los Angeles, Brandeis University, Amherst College, Howard University, Rutgers and Cornell University. Since 1980 up to the present, Sowell has worked at Stanford University's Hoover Institution. Here he hold a fellowship named after his mentor Rose and Milton Friedman.

Apart from his career in the academe, Sowell has also worked for think tanks like the Urban Institute. He was also a frequent guest at *Firing Line,* a show by William F. Buckley. Here he discussed the issues of privatization and the economics of race.

In 1990, Thomas Sowell was awarded by the American Enterprise Institute with the Francis Boyer Award. In 1998, the National Association of Scholars awarded him with the Sydney Hook Award. In 2002, Sowell was awarded with the National Humanities Medal for his 'prolific scholarship melding history, economics, and political science'. A year after, he was recognized for his intellectual achievement and he received the Bradley Prize. In 2004, his book *Applied Economics: Thinking Beyond Stage One* was recognized with the Laissez Faire Books' Lysander Spooner Award. In 2008, Sowell's book *Economic Facts and Fallacies* received the International Book Award from get Abstract.

Fireside Questions

"What would you do?"

Tip: These questions can be a fun exercise as it spurs creativity among the readers by allowing alternate scene endings and "if this was you" questions.

question 21

When he was young, Sowell's intelligence qualified him for a prestigious academic high school in New York City, Stuyvesant High School. However, when he was 17 years old, he was forced to drop out because of financial and domestic difficulties. What opportunities are available nowadays for bright minds like Sowell's that weren't accessible during his time?

~ ~ ~

question 22

Sowell's initial choice for a university was Columbia University. He wanted to study under George Stigler, a recipient of the Nobel Prize in Economics. However, when he learned that George Stigler already moved to the University of Chicago, he decided to follow him there. Why was it important for Sowell to learn from a particular man?

~~~

~~~

question 23

Thomas Sowell is a frequent guest at *Firing Line,* a show by William F. Buckley. Here he discussed the issues of privatization and the economics of race. What is Sowell's opinion on the issue of privatization?

~~~

question 24

While Sowell worked in Washington D.C. in civil service position, he attended the night classes at Howard University. What does this say about how Sowell gives importance to education?

~~~

question 25

Thomas Sowell has authored a lot of books since 1971 up to the present. One of his books is entitled *The Einstein Syndrome: Bright Children Who Talk Late*. Why are late-talking children frequently misdiagnosed with autism? What were Thomas Sowell's findings?

~~~

~~~

question 26

Transportation companies have fought against the laws of segregated seating but they lost. Some companies tried to ignore the law but when they were faced with fines, they began to comply. If you were the owner of the transportation company, will you quickly obey the law or will you challenge the law?

~~~

~~~

question 27

The academe will be at the forefront when it's popular to discriminate against blacks. They will also be at the forefront when what's popular to do is to discriminate in favor of blacks. If you were a university professor, will you also go with what's popular? Or will you stand with what you believe?

~~~

question 28

Sowell says that the difference between the white politicians and other segregationists from the white transportation owners was the transportation company owners would shoulder the cost of alienating the black riders and the former would not. If you were the transportation company owner, how would you respond to a law that would significantly decrease your profit?

~~~

question 29

In the year 2000, a study conducted by the U.S. Commission on Civil Rights showed that 44.6 percent of mortgage requests of black applicants were rejected. But only 22.3 percent of white applicants were turned down and 12.4 percent for Asian and native Hawaiians. If you were a black applicant whose mortgage was declined, how would you respond to this statistic?

~~~

~~~

question 30

Sowell writes about the Gujaratis and how they were expelled from Uganda. Many of the Gujaratis who arrived in Britain were once destitute but they stood up again and rose to prosperity. If you were a Gujaratis, how would you soar past your situation and prosper in a foreign land?

~~~

Quiz Questions

"Ready to Announce the Winners?"

Tip: Create a leaderboard and track scores to see who gets the most correct answers. Winners required. Prizes optional.

quiz question 1

Sowell writes about the tragedies created for the pursuit of social justice. He writes about the a group of people that was expelled from Uganda. What is this group of people?

~ ~ ~

quiz question 2

Data was gathered from Germany, Britain and United States that showed that the average IQ of firstborns is relatively higher than the average IQ of the siblings that came after them. The participants of this study were finalists of what competition?

quiz question 3

In the year 2000, a study conducted by the U.S. Commission on Civil Rights showed that 44.6 percent of mortgage requests of black applicants were rejected. Which ethnicity received the lowest percentage of disapproval of mortgage?

quiz question 4

One of the false myths is that if not for discrimination, everyone will be represented proportionately in various socio-economic characteristics. What are the different socio-economic factors?

quiz question 5

True or False: The Cubans who fled Cuba and came to the United States did not fare as well as the Gujaratis. There are fewer opportunities for the Cuban people in America compared to the Gujaratis in Britain.

~~~

quiz question 6

True or False: A study conducted by the U.S. Commission on Civil Rights in the lending industry showed that half of the mortgage requests of Asian applicants were rejected. But only 20 percent of black applicants were turned down.

~~~

~~~

quiz question 7

True or False: During the time when there was segregated seating on particular municipal transit companies in the South, many companies have fought against the laws but they lost. Some companies tried to ignore the law but when they were faced with fines so they began to comply.

~~~

~ ~ ~

quiz question 8

In 1958, Thomas Sowell received his Bachelor's
Degree in Economics from _____. He
graduated with the honors of magna cum laude. In
1959, he studied in Columbia University for his
Master's degree.

~ ~ ~

~~~

quiz question 9

In 1968, Thomas Sowell graduated from
_____ and received his Doctor
of Philosophy degree in Economics. His doctoral
dissertation was entitled *Say's Law and the General
Glut Controversy*.

~~~

~~~

quiz question 10

Thomas Sowell's book *Applied Economics: Thinking Beyond Stage One* was recognized with the Laissez Faire Books' Lysander Spooner Award. In 2008, Sowell's book _____ received the International Book Award from getAbstract.

~~~

~~~

quiz question 11

True or False: In 2002, Thomas Sowell was awarded with the National Humanities Medal for his 'prolific scholarship melding history, economics, and political science'. A year after, he was recognized for his intellectual achievement and he received the Bradley Prize.

~~~

quiz question 12

True or False: Young Thomas Sowell was intelligent and he qualified for a prestigious academic high school in New York City, Queens High School for the Sciences at York College. However, when he was 17 years old, he was forced to drop out because of financial and domestic difficulties.

~~~

Quiz Answers

1.   Gujaratis
2.   National Merit Scholarship
3.   Asians and Hawaiians
4.   Career, education, income, and incarceration
5.   False
6.   False
7.   True
8.   Harvard University
9.   University of Chicago
10. *Economic Facts and Fallacies*
11. True
12. False

Ways to Continue Your Reading

EVERY month, our team runs through a wide selection of books to pick the best titles for readers and reading groups, and promotes these titles to our thousands of readers – sometimes with free downloads, sale dates, and additional brochures.

[Click here to sign up for these benefits.](#)

If you have not yet read the original work or would like to read it again, you can purchase the original book here.

Bonus Downloads
*Get Free Books with **<u>Any Purchase</u>** of* Conversation Starters!

Every purchase comes with a FREE download!

Add spice to any conversation
Never run out of things to say
Spend time with those you love

Get it Now

or Click Here.

Scan Your Phone

On the Next Page...

If you found this book helpful to your discussions and rate it a 4 or 5, please write us a review on the next page.

Any length would be fine but we'd appreciate hearing you more! We'd be very encouraged.

Till next time,

BookHabits

"Loving Books is Actually a Habit"